prakṛti

---

nature's nature

me non we

For

My Father
who answered the question,

Where do we belong?

Smiling at me he pointed at the
trees-flowers-butterflies-birds-grass
and said,

'We're born out of nature,
to it we will return,
that is our nature!'

Acknowledgement

Being my first book, it is bound to have its share of flaws in parts, that I may have overlooked while compiling the whole. I appreciate your novelty in exploring the ideas of an author unknown and also request you to walk with me on this journey of *discovering nature* by enjoying, as well as, where required, taking a critical note of what could have been done better. The path of a writer can only become a meaningful ony if you, the reader, are able to comprehend and contribute to the concepts/verses put forth in this compilation. In this regard, I consider this book as an initiation to open up discussions through which we can enhance each other in becoming our own better selves.

This book is a convergence of many events and of primary essence is the enlightening interactions that I have had over the years with my brother, friends and strangers I have met during my travels. To take credit for it alone would mean to not acknowledge their *opening doors*, or me to walk through them. One of the most important of such doors that opened for me was into this world, through my Mother. I thank her and all of you for being a part of this ongoing odyssey.

For feedback and discussions : *rachanaprayana@gmail.com*

In[Con]tent

The eternal dawn
what (birds) spoke?
droppings of a little angel
her eyes
raining reality
tears of nature
infinite; is of water
a fenced horse
unicorn; a horse born
nadabrahma
Silence discovered

Life in a city
dialogues with yonder
'mist'ified
valley below
the fall
on a pooram night
everything is; in the making
Oh stranger! let us be nature's ranger

*The searching stork
does the ocean meet the sky?
me and sun's bind
goodbye sun! wish you could stay
the fiery and the fairy
beyond the waves
Crucified! in and by the ocean*

*Winter twilight
all about today evening
unorchestrated orchestra
firefly, will you take me high?
echoes of the night
who knew what lay ahead
discreet conversations*

*Care to stare
plethora of manifestations
...for boundaries, she didn't create
nature of creation
one with no origin
What should be left behind?*

PROLOGUE

The nature of being, more precisely, nature of existence have been contemplated from time immemorial. The forms this question has taken itself spanned multitudes of manifestations. There have been religions, metaphysics, science and so on, seemingly varied entities but attempts to address the age old, Who am I? How do I relate to everything? I understand that to bring down different lines of questioning to two is grossly narrowing their diversity but consider this as only an origin of a river that branches down to many tributaries. This path is taken to create a sense of direction in which this anthology of poems are going to navigate.

Whether we choose to agree or not, individually or collectively, the idea that Man(humanity as a whole) was/ is fascinated by the *Unknown* cannot be contested. The few who did venture out into the darkness have become pillars of the various manifestations we alluded to in the beginning. They were given pedestals or they found themselves on it, from which they proclaimed the Universal Truth'. Here we all stand, facing the 'Truth' they've claimed is 'Universal', asking ourselves, *What Truth?* and *Whose Truth?* The different paths taken by these (wo)men to make way or clear the way for humanity to bring us closer to the truth have in itself been so diverse that an individual at their adolescence(or whenever they decide that their curiosity outweighs security) is bound to experience conflict. This is not always external in nature, as there exists in our society or any society or culture, for that matter, conditioning of the human mind. The induction of individuals into a society through the current system of education is so narrow and limiting that it becomes hard for an individual to find meaning for their existence.

Knowledge, in and as itself, is a limiting process but in today's world our focus relies heavily on that. There are things that we can know for certain and there are those for which no amount of knowledge can be enough to take us to a logical conclusion in any meaningful way. The nature of nature is one such expedition and as such in corollary, the nature of life. In this context, all the various manifestations could(should) be considered as concepts to understand or elaborate the nature of 'Unknown'. These different traditions, although bound within their own cultural/historic backgrounds, strive for Universality(Universal Truth). This is where Nature comes to our assistance. Everything man has built so far, the civilizations that flourish in the 21st century has all been sprung from their own natural elements. The nature provides background for whatever development man has created or built but as is human nature of ingratitude, we get used to nature easily and we take it for granted quickly. The materialistic world has at its capitalist root the essence of what has been, over years, misconstrued as happiness - *desire.*

This *desire* is what we in today proclaim as the *Pursuit of Happiness.* Ask a (wo)man, Are you happy? They might say to the questioner's face, 'I am' while their inside will be burning to lay hands on the beautiful watch, or sunglasses or anything that they don't possess right now. This desire in its entirety is not to be blamed or at fault. It is something Nature worked hard to put into us while we were evolving, the desire to be better, the desire to be a better human being than we were yesterday, only today money measures it what once was measured by values. Our perverted imagination took us far away from that distant land of Self, from *being a better me*, it now has become *being better than the other*, far from ourselves and Mother Nature. Today, we turn to others to describe who we are, we look up to people to tell us who we could be while forgetting who we should be!

Nature is where the answers come in abundance. Nature is where everything is novel. Nature is where the journey of discovery is initiated. Nature is where we let go of our notions and conditioning about time. Nature is where the questions of 'Self' and our 'humanity' can be answered. The only way for us to trace back the path towards that ocean(**Verses by the Ocean**) of bliss that we left behind in search for 'better lives' is to **Find our Silence** and hear the **Call of the Wild**. Let her guide us, let the wind whisper in our ears, the sun light the path, the birds sing the forgotten songs of the past, hear that **Symphony of the night** that takes care of our tired bodies, let the moon wash us in its soothing glow, let us be free and experience the freedom that Nature has ensured that we were born into, after all this world is **Of her, not us.**

FINDING MY SILENCE

*Into the green I went
Within it, myself I lent,
to return to the **world of nature**
from that was **born my nature***

THE ETERNAL DAWN

An ethereal quality
does the eternal dawn has,
filled with myriad birds,
some flying - some gliding

The endless conversations
by the nocturnal crickets,
Do they really converse?
or simply woe a mate?

Also persistent in talking
are the crows and squirrels,
not to mention the buzzing mosquito
louder than the mobile alarm

From within the home
came the lizard's hissing
'Don't forget me,
I'm here too.'

In the temple distant, Gods
were being brought back to life,
but why do we think they sleep?
aren't they beyond human conceptions

Ah, that debate of God's existence
can indeed go on for ever
neither can I convince
nor will he evince

A waking man, now,
feels disturbed by nature's voices,
he and his puny vices
disonnected him from his own nature

His industrial mind
haven't slept in a while
as that body of his, is as tired
and longs, to belong in nature

Human ego though believes the opposite
compelling day after day,
throw himself unto work,
losing the quality of mind and body

Passing throught the valley
of, ever misinterpreted, Time
he pushes the limits of
his own existence

Waking up from his slumber
and walking in to this life
he doesn't feel this infinite, eternal dawn
but succumbs to *finitude of clocks*

WHAT (BIRDS) SPOKE?

Coming out in to the open
I was greeted by the rustling morning breeze
Closing my eyes, I could sense
the music, creation of wind and leaves

Coming to me from all around
What was beyond ignoring,
was all the melodious chirpings
from so many, of the sky's little angels

Flying from tree to tree,
how I wished I was free
to see life, as they see.

The colourful and musical melange
infused in me a renewed zest for life
Pigeons, fiery red eyes and claws
were calm and gathered on well and under roof

Crows, our ancestors, as is belief,
were already at top of caw's for morning rice
Sparrows, nimble, as they are
didn't stagnate, moving from place to place

Black drongo, lone and perched atop a tree
was a refined silhouette against the sky
Racket tailed drongos, the couple were animated,
a sight to behold, was their distinctive long tails

Magpie robin, an unexpected visitor of the lot
came and went, from and into nowhere
Yellow oriole, holding this canvas together
was the brightest spot in the morning sky

As my eyes moved from, birds to trees
the colourful, leaves, butterflies and dragonflies
feeling suspended in this celestial spectacle
I came to realize, in all this, I, the human, was a debacle

DROPPINGS OF A LITTLE ANGEL

In her own inactivity
she observed human activity,
should have been captivating,
the coming to life
of a species bound by time -
albeit having the possibility of transcendence
I wonder what she wonder,
her activity seems so casual
Where then did *we* lose to causal?
the descending mist, so far mystical
changed nothing, her search continued
the never-ending search for food

I looked at her in my inactivity
There is not any pretence
in her daily chores
What she think,
I don't know whether she think not,
she act out,
still there is so much room
for interpretations on her actions
what attracted me the most
is the subtle feathers
even more, the beautiful features
those small wings
carrying an agile body
moving around swiftly
adhered to no conformity,
her journey took them to places

So where did I go wrong?
What was it I should learn from her?
That would make my actions effortless
taking me forward in life
irrespective of time and space

It would suffice, if I
could get a fleeting glimpse
of her reality
That casual devoid of causal
I would tread ever so lightly
on my path, without bothering nature.

HER EYES

Through my eyes, I see
a world around her and me
She didn't look at me
maybe afraid of what she'll see

I didn't want to hurt her
I could see, not her too,
but so much has happened too,
If she flew away, I do understand her.

RAINING REALITY

An impending darkness - looms
Intermittent flashes - breaks
Following the deafening - crackling
of thunder, the sky beholds

There is a screen, evident now
through which I see,
the world somehow
changes not, it is what it was

Wind, at times, carry the drops away
the slant in drops playing out like a ballet
Sounds, I have heard before
plays now, a different tune

That bird I saw in the morning
now sings, hidden behind this screen
droplets - all over the floor
affects what I see and what not

There are valleys, for water
To flow and sow, but not to slow
As we vainly try,
To contain it in channels

The rain brought forth water
that left the sea and land,
To it, the water returns
remembering where it came from

TEARS OF NATURE

It was upon us, the hour of play
as we moved closer to end of the day
This time of day, always, nostalgic
acting on the mind as analgesic

The years moved backward
though in time we went forward,
to those good old days of childhood
that we try hard to hide in adulthood

A narrow alley awaited us
it doubled as a playground without fuss
the sun today, not too bright
from the west came a golden light

The leaves green, turned a shade light
Oh what a mesmerising sight!
In the east the day turned old,
silver clouds descending over the gold

Carrying in my hand, the cricket bat
I let go of myself and looked at that
the subdued sun in my face
behind me, the sky hiding its gaze

The feeling had crept in, of being a child
right before it was going to be exiled,
the innocent face was clouding
behind those eyes, childish joy was shrouding

The nature, it seemed was about to cry
it seemed, until its throat go dry
tears of joy or sadness I know not
in my own throat I felt a knot

throwing away the bat and the game
which to me was now lame,
I sat down and stared at everything
as a kid who could hear nature sing

The sun waved to me farewell
'feel it!', he forgot not to tell
the first drops of water, my body it caressed
I remembered his words, feeling blessed

It dawned on me, in this dusk
Life was not to be lived in brusk
The downpour was on its way
I stayed, waiting for it to take me away

What was happiness? I had asked
the tears on me and earth lay unmasked
there was no *happy* or *sad* in specific
all it carried was an emotion, pacific

So was also the crying kid
failing in its attempt to bid
for that immediate moment's bliss,
taken away from it, everything felt amiss

The mother nature whispered in my ears
'Stay and let me wash your tears,
listen, eternal, is not of joy and sorrow
live in today as there's no 'morrow'

INFINITE IS OF WATER

Water, wherever it fell
reflected its origin
also, had a story to tell

On leaves, their types, myriad
in some, the drop remained such
others, like this write, formed triad

On tiny branches, turned them animate
oscillating up and down
as nature opened heaven's gate

On trees, the wood absorbed
what it could, some the gravity took
on the surface, the rest lay, adsorbed

On birds, it turned them playful
evident from all their flying around
To human eyes, nothing more graceful

On earth, the pool turned muddy
yet it forgot not, to reflect the sky
calling to us, in its complexion, ruddy

On concrete, it became clear
as we've separated us from nature
away from nurture, year after year

The rain, intending to subside
felt the breeze lifting my self
taking the body with spirit, outside

On everything, we assume is of shapes
the water, we see, follows their form,
but, beyond our perceptions, it escapes

On body, water cleansed the skin
inside, where the spirit reside,
It was time for the journey to begin.

A FENCED HORSE

Along the rail
went the long trail,
through the green forest
I biked with a renewed zest

In the small villages
Time had had paused for ages,
There, the meadows so green
in a pasture was seen, a lone horse

He was looking into my eyes
without uttering a word, we said our *Hi's*,
We talked about earth and sky
and his journey and my

Wherein he confessed
A life confined, wasn't one he processed
Almost wept, *'Why the fences?'*
I apologized, *'We're out of our senses.'*

The trail wasn't at an end
further, it turned around the bend
Hidden behind the rows of apple tree
lay beyond, a nature wild and free

Into the green I went
within it, myself I lent
To return to a world of nature
from that was born my nature.

UNICORN; A HORSE BORN

Walking along the well laid trail
I heard a horse neigh, from down below
standing next to a retaining wall
One he couldn't climb, not with his legs tied
Did he see me?
Did he feel my presence?
not knowing either,
we stood there, face to face
he didn't neigh anymore
took me back to a Bowie song,
'... you're face to face
with the man who sold the world.. '
Not sure whether I was
He looked away,
rooted to place I stood,
wondering, *What stops him*
from taking off on a whim?
Watching him closer
my thoughts began to wander
How does he forget his strength
If not, why not see the rope?
What if he was not born to be a horse?
How did we come to imagine about unicorn?
Now he looks at me,
Now I see, he see me
his expression gave all the impression
Of what I and we did was wrong
He was not to be tied or tried
to a post or a wall,

born to be free,
destined to roam the hills
feeling the wind and its chills,
giving meaning to a life
that was to be well lived,
Unfortunately, stagnates in this corner
because of somebody's *free will,*
There it is, thought couldn't be free
just like he, from *free will,*
whether his own or man's
I can't seem to understand yet,
Will he ever get to become a unicorn?
Only time will tell!

NADABRAHMA

treading lightly, fingers-
palm - wrist - elbow - arm -
shoulder - chest - waist -
hip - thigh - knee - foot -
body - mind - ego - conscious
the music flowed through,
me not making any tunes
the music creating itself

I'm ignorant in the beginning
going along yet holding back strong
doubtful if this is the right song
but in a moment of silence,
I flowed - floated - lay suspended
a freedom I rarely felt

I let the creation take over
just a vessel, not anymore full
The emptiness resonating
louder in that silence,
with the *conscious* takeover,
I dropped my *cautious overlay* over

The questions never ceased,
Am I good enough?
Can I play like them, the Greats?
Will I be any better?
Now I was not on the banks,
the ever flowing river took me in

Not only my mind,
also the body united, *in sync*
songs of the birds reverberating,
in this hollowness,
coming forth was the sound of music
music that was creation itself
that was not searching anything
anymore, than the river reaching the ocean
neither beginning nor the end

This was the vibration that I felt
the vibration that I am
this is what we all are
this is what the universe is,
nadabrahma

SILENCE DISCOVERED

Had heard it over million times
the seemingly improbable myth,
finding that *inner peace,*
Surely I had to find first,
what it means to be *at peace*
in retrospective, thought had found them
during vacations when I was in nature,
unwinding myself from the confinement
of expectations and appropriations,
away from the society, away from
what everyone else wanted me to be

Only, nobody told me this
also, now I know, nobody can tell me this
neither can I, to you nor you to anyone

The birds do lend me their company
in the mornings, they wake me up
through the day, I hear them singing
to me and to anyone else who listened
it did take me time to notice
they didn't expect anything in return
I wondered why?
Why would they be so selfless?

The butterflies too
their short lived beauty
intensified my perception of colours
wanting to seek, what would they like

I moved in closer
Only to realize, I scare them

All of them flying away at my approach
The seeker in me hit a dead wall
with time, through these expeditions
No more I got any close
they were sure to fly away,
choosing to let my gaze follow
their maze, movements of head and flight

I came to a still, while my eyes
trailed their wings
In that stillness I could see the leaves
dark and textured over,
light and veins protruding, under
just like my palm - my fingerprints
and the natural order of things

I remember the illustration
of a peachy little bird on a toneless backdrop
by the artist Eiko Ojala,
perched atop a human finger
titled, *I found my silence,*
standing amongst these beauties
I discovered mine!

CALL OF THE WILD

Looking at me, my friend asked
'What's our purpose that lay masked?'
staring at the fall of water, slow
'Isn't purpose in the flow?'

LIFE IN A CITY

I've lived in a city,
long enough to imbibe
what the city transcribe
in that urbane vibe,
From that materialistic complicity

That of money I encountered,
while hiring a rental
he asked a price monumental
which I thought was urbane incidental,
Part of all the life's in the city I entered

The guy had a story to tell,
why he prefers to work independent
not the Uber corporate dependent
still he considers his life resplendent,
There began understanding of the city as a cell

'Why shouldn't a city develop?' asks my friend,
isn't that a good question?
It has to accommodate the pulsation
of the growing population,
What is it then we could amend?

People's gaze hardly meet,
Why don't we trust each other?
Why don't we do this together?
Why do we alienate the other?
Why not look up from our feet?

What is stopping me from talking,
about the things in my mind's wandering
about my innermost heart's pondering
neither do you tell what you're wondering,
Can't we all be together in this walking?

Tell me an idea and I'll tell you mine,
only if you ask me what's in my mind
not that of the materialistic kind
let's talk about an idea we can find,
Can't it then be seen all our life's will be fine?

Parted ways with my friend on the road,
went to the market as I was sold
had to spent some of that hard won gold
because that's what everyone's being told,
They say, come unload your boatload

Almost everything around, made me an offer,
that was hard for me to refuse
an ideology I was to infuse
even if they all confuse,
To keep coughing up from my coffer

On my way back, saw in the street,
the part of city's heart beat
few kids achieved that feat
some real flesh on the meat,
Passing around the ball with their feet

The evening breeze brought with it,
through its breezy sound
talks about lives not bound
We all can still be found,
of the truth that we all fit

City or village it doesn't matter,
let us be honest to ourself
Isn't that the best way to lift oneself
Why not value life for itself,
Let us take each other beyond chatter

This is not an epiphany,
maybe a simpleton mind's nonsense
not meant as any offense
that's all I've in my defense,
Why not strive for a life of symphony?

DIALOGUES WITH YONDER

On those closed eyelids
he felt the rays,
Through the window pane
in did they came

Was he sleeping
or laying aware?
nevertheless, the light stirred in him
something pure and bright

Why did he chose
to keep his eyes closed?
Was it fear
of blinding the eyes, so dear?

Had he opened, he could've seen
The dancing silhouettes,
by leaves and branches
of the trees in the meadow

Were they trying to speak
in a language they know,
an inherent response
to that eternal flow?

Was it he who was lost?
When he ventured inland
from that shore he landed
centuries and millenniums ago

Round and round
The merry of life goes
extantly, he knows not nor sees
That merry, he felt on the shore,
looking back at the sea,
Was the ferry of adventure, that left

The sun is fading,
into the incoming darkness
He doesn't feel the light
not anymore on his shut eyes

Is he not able
to trace back those footprints,
that he left on his way here?
To wake himself up
from his sleep,
that doesn't allow the light
nor etched forms on the window pane
As he forgot the language
of his own *dialogue with yonder*

'MIST'IFIED

A cool breeze welcomed my face
the space, my room, as I left behind,
the chirping of birds was audible too
figuring out the way east
to watch that, awakening sun, rise
Walking towards the hill
was not sure of the path,
Some were laid with technology
others lay well-beaten,
the movement of man and animal
paved the way I was taking,
Think it was only a natur(e)al choice,
The climb up, began easy
the views were rewarding
hills stepping down in distance
was how, here, nature defined itself,
The overhanging white clouds,
the sun shining behind
was at the heart of it,
I became still, an observer
images of similar landscape
from wherever I have been before
opened in my mind, spatial and temporal portals
transfixed nevertheless transported
i was brought back by a call from within,
'..let us move on, the journey has to go on...'
The hill welcomed with a ringing bell,
a reminder of the sanctity
just like it is when entering a Temple,

The hill, all of sudden became
intensively alive with life and death
towards the east, downhill, to some distance
the trees were of thick foliage
losing it along the way
gradually turning thick grey
Sitting under the shade I saw
the white clouds so thick and bright
yet transforming into flimsy mist
as they came closer,
The landscape with all its varied forms,
shapes and life, approaching slowly,
losing its multiplicity
becoming a unified, subtle white
This whole with all it's underlying glory
took in, myself, like the hill,
engulfing me within its inherent unity.

VALLEY BELOW

Deep down, there exists a valley below
too deep, for light to reach often
It so happens, *when it snows inside*
The light reflects from all the peaks
going all the way down, illuminating
the source of all projections
that we all see and believe, are
disconnected events, connected
only to the passage of time
What if, we appeal to *the Self*, start connecting?
I, the ego, am tired of collecting

The coincidences, we think
are simply miracles of life
Why not, look from where we stand
to the valley below
Aren't all these hills connected
by and to this valley?
Then how can the projections
and all the epiphanies in life
be different and not a part of *our being?*

All these different peaks we create
are only expressions of this bedrock
My want and my need are in constant conflict
My want, to scale all the possible peaks
My need, to walk me down to *the Self*
and show me all that I can be
And not what others tell what I should be

The lit path now I walk
to the core of need, forgetting want
no more does my ego hurt
The choice it has made, to itself hurl
to reach the valley before the snow recede
From there to look up and learn,
what in life, precede
Now, I know, I don't want to succeed,
nor any expectations of the society, I will exceed

In this journey I'll look at me
maybe, afraid of what I'll see
nevertheless, until I reach that valley
I can't really see,
once I reach there
I'll walk my life's alley.

THE FALL

All these human voices
are nothing but noises,
What did the falling water say
was a needle lost in the hay

I knew it was there
couldn't be found, even when laid bare,
Why did we chose to see
this beauty, through this camera key

The water kept coming down
around the stones in a marriage gown,
The leaves of that green fern
adorned the gowns pleats

Raised their arms and took selfies
some random stranger made it groupies,
How can it not be then
felt nothing, these women and men

Looking at that lone stone
I wondered how was it born,
between the valley and hills
Nature bestowed its drills

Looking at me my friend asked
'What's our purpose that lay masked?'
staring at the fall of water, slow
'Isn't purpose in the flow?'

ON A POORAM* NIGHT

Does he see me like I see him?
amongst the crowd
I'm here, but why?
The music being produced
I'm familiar with it
Yet for no reason I wonder,
Why is he staring at me?
I hear it often
during the hottest season,
Born to be in the wild
but here I am, brought in by humans
Am I not to wonder then,
Why not while it's cold?
As usual, the music picks up
The atmosphere is charged
But don't they see, I don't enjoy it!
again our eyes meet ,he seems to see me,
That is rare but he can't do anything
They come and go
The ones with who I think
We can communicate
Nothing has and nothing will
change ever until they see me
Like he and others does,
not through their eyes
Just from within,
Do they even know I don't
or ever won't
Know what they want me to do

A festival in Indian state of Kerala celebrated in temples with elephants

Even with all their actions!
I think, they think, they know,
All I do feel is that long rod
hitting in me in all the wrong spots,
if I am to show my irritation,
Isn't it right to feel pain?
Oh but what do I know,
I'm but just an elephant, an animal
emotions are for humans!

EVERYTHING IS; IN THE MAKING

Looking around, I asked myself
Who am I to judge
anyone or anything?
I don't even know,
where do I stand, in my own land
I can't help but notice,
forgive me, I'm only a novice

Nature tells stories,
everyday, everything; in creation-
in coming to life - in creating life
in being life - in manifestating life,
the sapling I planted yesterday
is a plant today,
is becoming a tree tomorrow

The day is in the making of night
night is in the making of the day
the leaves in today, so green
turns yellow or red without preen,
from it, the flower sprout minute,
metamorphose into fruit, every minute

me and you, if only we want,
can see how we collect wont,
not along lines of nature, of us or nature
rather upon experiences we nurture
If we confess that to self, one day
we can begin, learning life from next day

becoming an observer, what we do -
how we act and react - what we say -
how we feel - all of this simply see,
look at us objectively,
The boundaries blur, between you and me

you're looking at me and you,
the whole of humanity in you and me
How then can we fail to see?
that, as in nature,
We all are in the becoming - to be

Onwards, life leaves
one of two choices,
one that was revealed well,
in Hamlet's hell,
through Shakespeare's quill it fell,
to be or not to be!

OH STRANGER, LET'S BE NATURE'S RANGER

People say things they don't mean
They mean what they don't say
I say things I don't know
I know things yet I don't say
Wherein then lies our decay?

Tell me this, between you and me
What's this gulf we don't see
Oh I feel it, so do you

As a father, you know me
about this life, you teach me
But if you impose things on me
I'll fly away, certainly, from thee

As a child, I know you
taught me love, another word for - Mother
brought me forth, into light, from you
I came alive, dear mother,
as the morning drew, like a morning dew

as a sibling we fought together
at times, each other,
in the evening as we gather,
as siblings, mother and father
we forgive one another

In being friends, we all flourished
each other's soul we nourished

the moments that we all cherished,
with those our home were furnished

If you and I know this, my dear granger
neither you nor me, are in danger
Let us be our and nature's ranger
Why not try this for a change, oh stranger?

VERSES BY THE OCEAN

Letting myself unwind
for the body to find,
its own waiting mind
shedding light on me and Sun's bind,
no more I felt confined
becoming one with mankind!

THE SEARCHING STORK

Walking with a sway
while being as much gay,
She was searching in the day
for the day's hay

There was bending down,
the neck, from the white gown,
the yellow beak pecking light brown,
expressing no frown

Least bothered by her quest,
completely forgetting her zest
barged in a few uninvited guest,
Strangely, she didn't consider them pest

She took off in a short flight
without putting up a fight,
Don't suppose she was fright
maybe, wanted to stay away from sight

Nevertheless, she continued, again
not bound by any chain,
her search for the grain,
without leaving, on the beach, any stain

While in the name of food
mankind has destroyed all the good,
Slowly burning away the edges of wood
Unsettling everything under the nature's hood

Hope one day we would see
How a Stork does, the nature, see
once destroyed, there's nowhere to flee
Let us wake up from our ignorant glee!

DOES OCEAN MEET THE SKY?

Far away, as far as my eyes can go
there seems to be a line,
not as much as a line
but a darkening of the ocean's colour

Where the hues of light turn dark
The ocean alone does that
The sky remains what it was
Do they meet though?

If I'm to believe my eyes
They kiss each other,
for eternity, if that's what *always* is
But I once heard, *don't believe what eyes see!*

The waves do grumble
yet touches the sand softly,
Leaving a pattern on them
just as they're are, wavy

The bluey hue turns white
as the ocean comes closer to the sight,
Oh the colours of nature!
A human can't possibly nurture

I'm not lost for words, not now
I'm lost in the waves,
are they an orgasmic truth
of the love of Ocean and Sky?

Beyond this cornucopia of waves,
their thrashing on the beach,
there is a peace that speak
about the love affair of nature

That nature of nature, I vainly describe
insofar as my language can,
even so, I know it fails
To tell the truth about their meeting place

There can't exist a line of meeting
It is what man has created - *horizon*
To see, to know, to feel and understand
how nature plays games with us.

ME AND THE SUN'S BIND

The moment was right
Sun was not, anymore bright

The me wanted to know
What the mind knew somehow

Looking at the sun
I asked him, *'Where's the fun?*

To come and go, around the clock
don't you feel in the lock?'

I suppose he smiled, the breeze whispered,
'Shouldn't you feel at ease?'

Feeling the water relaxing my body,
also doing the work was *toddy* *

'Look around the nature wild and free
but, sadly, you work around me.'

Letting myself unwind
for the body to find,
its own waiting mind
shedding light on me and Sun's bind,
no more I felt confined
becoming one with mankind!

**An alcoholic drink made from coconut tree*

GOODBYE SUN, WISH YOU COULD STAY!

Thank you for the day
I know, can't do it enough,
You take care of the world
I'm only part of the whole
yet you shine not only for the world
but for every individual
as they all see you
and enjoy the life you give

Thank you Sun!
I know you're bright
and I can't look at your light
shining star of the day,
In the evening you go red
the brightness turn light
Subtle is that dying light,
but now, we can look at each other

I would like to ask you
How was your day?
I don't know, how,
can you answer that
Here I sit, on the sandy shore,
looking at you going down
Would you mind
if I've another question to ask?

How do you do it everyday?
regardless of our ingratitude

We don't thank you anymore
neither acknowledge your charity
if you're bright, we do complain,
if you're not, we still complain
If not here somewhere else
You hear that all,
Ignoring, still shine bright
Giving away all the life

Thank you Sun!
for what I'm able to do, the fun
It's all because of you
Your grace and your presence
today I wish I didn't have to see
you going down the horizon
Extending my hope, to have a talk
also an evening walk
to learn gratitude
as I've forgotten that attitude.

THE FIERY AND THE FAIRY

With the wind against our faces,
we sat there with fixed gazes,
A spectacle of the day, unfolding,
that was what, we were beholding

Today, most clouds stayed away
but enough for the colours to sway
our sensory perceptions,
without any kind of deceptions

The day's light, glowing fiery red
On the sky's canvas, his bed
Oh what a beauty! the evening packed
filling everything that I lacked

The kites performed the sky-dance,
Waves produced for them, trance
That lone eagle hovered in the distance
unlike kite, without any assistance

Ocean met the sky over horizon
maybe there exists, a Zion
From down below, the atmosphere, gray
just above, reddish hue in full display

The creeping darkness crept in unnoticed
an ignorant me, only later, noticed
the sand beneath eroded away
yet, rooted in this sand I stay

Turning around, I saw the fairy,
blowing wind, setting an ambience so airy,
coming up amongst the silhouette of trees
expressing nature's manifestation in degrees

There seems nothing more I can say
to give an impression of the day,
Venus-rise bringing in twilight
To me, Nature said, *'It is going to be a good night!'*

BEYOND THE WAVES

Emanating from the darkness
beyond the existence of horizons,
The waves and stars,
doesn't speak about any mystery

Close your eyes listen to them
feel the sand beneath your feet,
The cool sea breeze on the face
Remember the long gone days.

The times as a child, becoming one with sea
not worried about the days of future,
Letting the water *au fait* the present
Without knowing what that meant

The constellations, always spoke
but I don't remember speaking,
The language I had forgot
with all that life brought

Now as I look up,
I always find Orion,
He confides in me on order
even when everything seem random

The sand I stand on,
When I look down
Shows me all the same
That *duality is lame!*

The wind whispers
Never be stagnant,
nothing is ever done
also life's *never gone*

The waves kept lashing
on the sands of the beach,
not to their wanting
but an *innate nature's calling*

Clouds appear and disappear
painting on the sky's canvas,
through them, are visible the stars
devoid of everything farce

Amongst all this I stay
on that known bay,
waiting for life to fray,
Ignoring the boat that lay,
I think it's time, not delay
to venture without foray
Feel life everyday
Before turning gray!

CRUCIFIED! IN AND BY THE OCEAN

The sky was too bright
The ocean, harsh,
that was how it was,
When I found myself crucified

A cork bobbing on the surface,
water pouring over my face,
couldn't open my eyes
neither close my nose

My hands too, were tied
strangely, by the tides,
drifting further away into ocean
carried by the homecoming waves

The silence was serene,
Leaving behind the human voices,
had no more inherent vices,
The moment, brought me back to life

Had believed all this while
crucifixion would take away life
In its stead, it reminded of my breath
across the body's breadth

All this mind could feel
was the pumping of my blood,
Inevitable it was I would bleed,
not blood, but my ego

There couldn't exist, not anymore
Me and Ocean as different *entities*
I was being led away
away from this shore, opening another door

One that existed when I was born
but one I've shunned for long
No more I couldn't meet my self,
I was the *Man Alone with himself* *

Title of Friedrich Nietzsche's book

SYMPHONY OF THE NIGHT

'Lighten up my dear child,
don't be afraid, darkness is not wild
Come to me, beginning twilight
we'll sing songs of the night,
You and me, we'll go on a ride,
on a journey to uncover what the night hide.'

WINTER TWILIGHT

The horizon glowed as remnant embers
of a day walking into the twilight,
as the snow's white receded into the dark

the light falling on hanging clouds;
a melange of orange and red
occupying the emptiness amongst trees

Staring at the crossroad lying ahead,
I stare at the abyss of incoming darkness
the landscape of mind, play out in nature

The silhouettes, carry no more leaves,
sentinels, watching over the earth
The nature hides its truth in plain sight
Isn't that obvious seeing the bright light?

The path ahead holds this *omnium gatherum,*
echoing the ethos of man's dilemma,
beings we are, finding ourseleves at intersections

The winter lights illuminates the snow's white,
from its core come forth, those rays of light
as the day walk into twilight,
I decided to follow this light

leaving behind the meeting of roads,
ready to accept the winter's cold
and a journey that cannot be foretold

ALL ABOUT TODAY EVENING

It is a starry sky,
Looking at the stars we lay by lay-by,
Orion was the easiest to find
Though Ursa major was on my mind

My friend began, blast from his past,
A moment moulded in time he cast
talking about a blinding light
In dark, could see the other's face so bright

The other mentioned the satellite
which, for me was like a fallen kite
The train in the distance hooted
a nostalgia that sound floated

Somebody said, *beedi* * is in the house
I silently hoped, is not bitten by the mouse,
That flashing red light of a plane
When will it land on that airport lane?

Unfortunately the electricity came
The present's serenity it maim,
Where to with this poem I wonder
In the world of thoughts it wander

That music of night, silence
finding in it my guidance
The orange light at the end of it
elevated the conscious a little bit

** An indian form of cigarette wrapped in a particular tree leaf*

Under the leaves now we sit
through the leaves we see the sky as lit,
I returned home on bike
for a distance not even worth a hike

Lying down on bed after dinner
by being late, Mother acts as if I'm a sinner
not wanting to get into a lovely fight
I said her to have a good night

Thinking out loud, noiseless
to let preach the dormant conscious, voiceless
drifting back to physicality casually
I stepped on the reality causally

Letting my eyes close to embrace the dark
from that pier, on my journey, I embark

UNORCHESTRATED ORCHESTRA

Only the light from the screen,
from this omniscient source, mobile,
a call from the wild, did keep coming
floating through to my ears,
The only time I really hear it,
was in between, when my eyes closed

As the light faded,
the call, I had been hearing,
switched into nature's voice,
Thus it, at once, began
as I focused on silence,
all I could hear was the music...

...they were a few, in the orchestra,
played by the grasshoppers
The closest one somehow knew
how to begin every note new,
it always was, the highest sound,
with other's behind, following his lead

lying down, with closed eyes,
I could feel their pulse
catching up with their rhythm
I left my thought's realm
Spirit stepping out of the body,
listening to them in the night's lobby

Why then was it unorchestrated,
You and I may introspect, wait,
as the conductor, paused the symphony,
The night was pervaded by harmony,
almost slipping into that peace
when I heard the master piece

A low, clear, high pitch voice,
was heard from further away,
He knew not that orchestra had ended,
He may have slept, his ways he mended
forgetting yet remembering where he belong
decided the moment he was up, to play along

He was not alone in his sleep
neither he nor I could recollect
where was it the music had stopped
Content was I, I was brought back to life
Sitting up straight, decided to hear the rest,
pulsating it was, when he played with zest

All it took though, for both of us to realize,
in a moment that did materialise,
He was the only one singing in the group
And I was the sole listener,
While I thanked him for my awakening
everybody stared at him, as he was the sinner.

FIREFLY, WILL YOU TAKE ME HIGH?

Oh my good old friend,
Yes it is time to, my ways, amend,
or choose to later lament
I'll tell you, it has been a torment,
now it's easier to see what you meant
It was, that, about what I always dreamt

'Firefly, will you teach me to fly?'
as a kid, I looked at the sky
You emerged, from the navy blue canvas,
shining and bright, the stars, flavours of flavus,
came out of their hiding from sunlight
lightening up the dark night

Tiring my little neck, with a frown,
my eyes traced you while coming down,
was sad couldn't hold on longer,
wished my neck was stronger,
that was when the world heeded my call
an angel from heaven, was your fall

The glowing light on your tail
held stronger, my head frail,
Curiosity got the better of me,
that's when I began to see,
brightening up my whole universe,
you sang the night's most beautiful verse

'Lighten up my dear child,
don't be afraid, darkness is not wild
Come to me, beginning twilight
we'll sing songs of the night,
You and me, we'll go on a ride,
on a journey to uncover what the night hide.'

Years later, in my today, I confide
I had forgotten, what you in me did confide,
running behind a day, others guide,
I let myself slide and glide
Now that you've come back,
or is it that life, to you, brought me back?

Let's find again our lost songs
Kindly let me right some wrongs,
Your wings had taken me high,
now I admit that with a sigh
Let's go back again into the nights
To find them higher lights

ECHOES OF THE NIGHT

On everything did it fall
On the way down its fall,
many a leaves were lit
as the night's fruit was lit,
through the trees profile
I saw the moon shone within its profile,
so was the sky, a tinted blue canvas
insofar; an impressionist canvas,
the stars here, as were everything, dots
trifling, yet the whole medley appeared in dots,
leaves in the shadow formed a silhouette
from trees that themselves were silhouette
there was in the distance a bright light,
an electric post that was in the night's light,
on the invisible rail tracks far away,
a locomotive took people miles away,
into distant destinations and far away land
In such a place I did land,
Looking out from this lair
I realize the truth of a lair,
the nocturnals whispered to the wind
Their voices reach me, carried by the wind,
Shadows on the ground laid in a pattern
only light and dark partaking in this pattern,
The silent voices of the day
comes alive in the night everyday,
My thoughts, not voice, taking the lead
wanting to know, *'Where they will lead?'*
'Oh my, Why?', the night questions

One of my own quintessential questions
'Why do you bother about morrow?
Isn't life in the now and future only morrow?'
darkness of night was the more wise
the silence was reflective as well as wise
A thought made my eyes close
only to see the darkness which was close
The *symphony of night* played along
carrying me further as I tagged along

WHO KNEW WHAT LAY AHEAD

The time, I feel had come,
it had been sometime
since the sensation has been rooting
to take flight into that night
Skeptic I was, I agree,
but you must forgive my cynicism
it was always against the mysticism
Yet here I was, on the road
leaving behind the habitual light
into the incoming darkness,
The beauty though, so happened
I had my comrades,
their camaraderie filled the car
the laughter kept coming in waves
This was how it was,
taking the road to the hills,
here the moon awakened
unbeknownst to our arrival
But greeted us the same
with all his grace
rising over the distant hill
we didn't recognise him
not atleast with his first light
just then one of us shouted,
'Fools, it's the moon!'
Now the silhouette of a tree
was so observed against his bright canvas
Again, forgive our excitement
We hadn't seen a moonrise like this

I stood there, spellbound by the Ursa major
I've to tell you a secret,
It has been sometime since we had talked
They're visibly upset
We used to converse in my childhood
I remember nights filled with amazement
When I stared at them and asked questions
about them and their neighbours,
Orion and Ursa minor, also
Why minor was called so?
Will tell you that story,
maybe some other time
As you heard before, here I stood
mending some broken relations
Orion smiled as he always did
not with lips but with a bend at his hips
It was time, *or was it?*
kindly forgive my ignorance
Please do tell me, why, it was time?
Everybody keep repeating it
What does it imply?
Isn't time an illusion, we created
to find coherence for existence?
How do I explain now, this
sensation that I'm feeling,
that there is no child me or adult me?
It was just me and them
Me and my conversations with Ursa Major
and Orion too, also moon but
he's busy dealing with clouds
as they devoured him
yet his aura shines through
So yes, in this moonlit kingdom
I don't feel no time

and in this darkness
Silhouettes are the messengers
they speak of no time, they stay same
they speak of possibilities,
one that of a journey, by the day
and of an eternal unity at night
As I get back behind the wheels
I hear the whispers in the wind
of a dialogue we all had
leading to the paths that lay ahead
before my ego is dead.

DISCREET CONVERSATIONS

Lying down, I look up
Up above the stars form a cup
Cup? You may wonder,
Wonder all you want, but I lie under
Under this nature's dialogue
Dialogue between the stars
Stars and the vast sky
Sky with dark silhouette of trees
trees do whisper to the wind
Wind laughs at this joke
Joke? You are sure to ask
Ask away and I'll duly tell
Tell I'll, because Why not?
'Not at all!' the tiny star responded
Responded to the brighter one
One that made fun, *'Aren't you dull?'*
Dull? tiny thought and said out loud,
Loud that others heard, *'Maybe,*
Maybe, I'm 'you' in the making!'
Making the brighter one a tad lighter
Lighter now, was also the sky
Sky though was indeed Sly
Sly why? Sky smiles, knowing why!
'Why are you smiling?' asked the tree
Tree was curious about the smiling sky
Sky had a nice reply without a lie,
'Lie these stars on my canvas,
Canvas is mine, yet one is proud of bright
bright he is, only while I stay dark!'

Dark I am too, the tree thought
Thought, shared by the whole, tree, lot
Lot of them dancing in what the wind brought,
Brought by the wind was a cool breeze
Breeze that shook the tree's darkness
Darkness in which wind was moving,
Moving in space, rustling the leaves
Leaves now murmured to the wind
'Wind, did you hear what the stars talked?'
Talked about the nature's dialogue with herself
Herself then took me in to the conversation
Conversation about every being's existence
Existence that should acknowledge creation
Creation of them and me and you
You then have to know this as well
Well, that's all I had to say in the end
About each and every night's beauty, my friend!

OF HER, NOT US

While my own,
sleep or work in the next room,
We look at each other
wondering about our differences

CARE TO STARE

Sitting on my chair
Pushing myself to cut my hair,
took me out of my lair
out into the fresh village air
I saw a beautiful mare
conversing with an animate hare
I found time, to share
a moment such rare
but not long enough to disrupt their,
Unnaturally natural, pair
I carried on with my affair
thoughts wandered to Voltaire
his perfection and the time we require.
Jolted back into reality by a glare,
A flash of light from the village square,
gave me a wild scare
though intending, to stare
encouraging myself to dare
At the least for the life I care
being knight with conscious as squire
and never to compare
On the journey to be aware
Optimistic, never to let this flare
die down or not treated fair.

PLETHORA OF MANIFESTATIONS

Of what can I not be conscious?
as though acting distant from past,
not at all detached from its clutches
I create my own trenches
In time, before I think, this moment is gone
Without my own company,
I miss it in a blink
On what plane am I to meet
That profound hidden trait
Is it called fate or natural state?
Who are you? I ask in vain
Why am I afraid, is it fear?
If so, will try to understand fear
Is it from known or unknown?

Why not analyse?

If known then why bother
What then could lie in the unknown?
Do you or I, or Can you or I, know?
If not, why don't we hear
that life's calling we all bear
If we now learnt to go beyond fear,
What is it then lie in next layer?
Maybe, could it be security?
That losing of familiarity
does there, lay my disparity?
Can we not see that plainly?
then why not go one up

Walking higher and higher
I push through each layer
I will now pause, it's necessary
to perceive beyond what I receive
quiet introspection, from this high
see all my misconceptions flew by

Look, how far we climbed,
through the layers, back at our mind
Something has changed hasn't it?
Doesn't the psyche transform, or
we still choose to be the same?
Further, the layers, are higher stacked
We know, we're not what we were then
Nor what we become tomorrow

Can then we see, *life as a perennial process?*
The essence of it, ever transience
yet, always does nurture our conscious

No more, then, could I define 'I', *the ego*
The 'I', transpose into the *abstract*
moulded by an epoch of conditioning

Once we, this concede,
There hardly exist, paths to recede,
Why? We know it'll impede
learning, none of our lives, over others, precede

Why not then set forth?
I ponder over, everything so far
feeling in me an ascent
onto that elusive clarity, about clarity
up and up, we can go

Into that land, overtly bright,
or excessively pitch black

Couldn't it be, that, that is an origin?
of creation and of life
inclusive in it, all the exemplification
and the very nature of every manifestation.

...FOR BOUNDARIES, SHE DIDN'T CREATE

Man built his home
with brick and mortar,
Creating boundaries
in his own space

Look at her, the tree,
what is it that binds
our existence here
At this very moment?

While my own,
sleep or work in the next room,
We look at each other
wondering about our differences

Man created architecture
One of three basic needs,
Food, clothing and shelter,
Protecting himself from nature

Wasn't it fear?
of what, known or unknown
We now know not,
but continue to be
afraid of something, naught taught

In through the frames, openings
Created in the wall
We see but do we observe?

bringing forth limited perception
Alas! unlimited preception

Bound by these fences,
we sowed a seed
and grow it did,
Not to our will
rather it heeded,
A call from within

The seed grew
into a sapling, little by little,
The roots spread,
stem sprouted the buds
into leaves and flowers
fruits hung from their umbilical cords

She couldn't be held down
to our puny vices,
Closing in on our selves,
leaving behind all traces

The causality of becoming,
meanwhile, blown asunder
unlike her, the tree
growing ignorant of the fences
Letting the passers-by
Pick the fruit of earth's labor.

NATURE OF CREATION

I know what is, to feel good,
but faced with, *What is good?*
I'm at loss for words to explain
the existence of that ex - plain
through that which I had moved,
while the world around constantly moved

Then there is evil, everyone claims they know,
but is there anything real there to know?
once something else we already know
confronts our present know,
Is there a real dichotomy between good and evil?
Isn't 'live' the anadrome of evil?

The root of good and evil, encapsulates,
that, every being from within, encapsulates
every element, possess this from nature
that is indeed every being's nature
Why is it hard to know this while I feel this?
My mind is always split by either that or this

This duality is inherent in every creation
I perceive, isn't that *fundamental to creation?*
How do I know what is better?
If I don't create something better?
And if I don't create anything at all,
How am I to know what was wrong after all?

There is no past or future status quo,
this moment now, is creation's quid pro quo,
What is creation taking away from my life?
My experience of living this life!
If then, isn't it my responsibility,
to approach and live a life with this responsibility?

ONE WITH NO ORIGIN

Where does it all begin?
in the beginning or the end?
at birth or at death?
Is the question cyclical or philosophical?

Life is all that's in between,
the beginning and the end
being born to walk into death,
Meanwhile, should I survive or thrive?

The new born I was,
Don't remember how it was
When I watch other kids cry
The last drops of memory goes dry

from child to adult did we grow
not bothered, yet with the flow
not knowing wrong from right
through it, learning what was right

An adult is the mature one
Who knows, what is to be done
or thinks they know for sure
while foregoing everything pure

We accumulate experiences
collected from all the senses
processed through prejudiced chambers
leaving novelty burning out as embers

This burning adulthood turn old age
We assume we've wisdom of a sage
Once again, ignoring our ignorance
we seek out some form of deliverance

Why are we habituated to forget
that the things over which, we fret
aren't always of the best kind
there are always better questions we can find

WHAT SHOULD BE LEFT BEHIND

What is the purpose?
my friends asks,
probably, more to himself
than to my own self
Who am I to answer?
To him or me?
'I don't know', I said,
out loud enough for him,
inside, burning with questions,
I confronted the question,
taking me back to a journey
when nature answered it,
Under the fall of water,
with a smile I heard her say,
'...purpose is the flow...'

I've felt it, I've said it,
the moment I try to define,
it slips like beach sand
from the palm of my tightly held hand
Whole of life, people,
events, things, science,
logic, thoughts, emotions
have defined a life, not sure
how else could it have been
until the nature held me,
shook me violently, awakening
me from a sleep so deep,
forgetting all what I was taught,

I observed nature without doubt
All I could say when it happened,
take me where you want,
Show me what I don't know
Tell me what I do know
It has been some time
since we have discussed,
Sun, sky, clouds,
Trees, leaves, fruits,
night, stars, moon

I've become detached
from you, from me, from everything
leading a mechanical life
amongst all this strife,
I've forgotten myself
Kindly show me my Self
If I'm to live in today
What should I leave for morrow
Or is it my yesterday?

I know I believe in memories
But they don't exist in future
Neither can be created in my past
So is it not in now, I should focus?
If I don't do it being aware,
Then why should I care,
Why do it at all?

Thank you, Mother nature, for the reminder
From now on I'll take care of remainder
I'll live to leave behind,
something of the worthy kind

www.ingramcontent.com/pod-product-compliance
Lightning Source LLC
Chambersburg PA
CBHW051216250726
48655CB00006B/2436